Reading American History

Pilgrims in America

Written by Melinda Lilly
Illustrated by Jonna Baruffi

Educational Consultants

Kimberly Weiner, Ed.D

Betty Carter, Ed.D

Rourke

Publishing LLC

Vero Beach, Florida 32963

www.rourkepublishing.com

This is for my family: A.J., Shay, Andie and Andrew
—J. B.

Designer: Elizabeth J. Bender

Library of Congress Cataloging-in-Publication Data

Lilly, Melinda.
  Pilgrims in America / Melinda Lilly; illustrated by Jonna Baruffi
      p. cm. — (Reading American history)
  Summary: Briefly presents the Pilgrims' 1620 trip from England to Massachusetts and what life was like after their arrival, including the feast of thanksgiving which they shared with the native people.
   ISBN 1-58952-360-1 (hardcover)
  1. Pilgrims (New Plymouth Colony)—Juvenile literature. 2. Massachusetts—History—New Plymouth, 1620-1691—Juvenile literature. [1. Pilgrims (New Plymouth Colony) 2. Massachusetts—History—New Plymouth, 1620-1691. 3. Thanksgiving Day. 4. Holidays.] I. Baruffi, illus. II. Title.

F68 .L73 2002
974.4'8202—dc21   2002001039

Cover Illustration: Pilgrims land in Massachusetts.

Printed in the USA

Time Line

Help students follow this story by introducing important events in the Time Line.

1565   Spanish colony at St. Augustine, Florida

1585   English colony at Roanoke, Virginia

1607   English colony at Jamestown, Virginia

1620   The Mayflower lands at Plymouth Rock.

1621   The First Thanksgiving is celebrated.

1624   Dutch colony at New Netherland

The **Pilgrims** want a new life in **America**.

The Pilgrims leave home.

The Pilgrims go to the ship,
the **Mayflower**.

At the Mayflower

In 1620, the Pilgrims cross the sea.

The Mayflower at sea

At last, the Pilgrims see land.

It is America!

A Pilgrim boy sees America.

The Pilgrims make homes.

A new home

There is not much food.

The Pilgrims get sick.

Sick Pilgrims at home

The **Native Americans** help the Pilgrims plant **corn**.

A Native American plants fish with the corn.
That will make good **dirt**.

Now, the Pilgrims have friends
and food.
The Pilgrims ask the Native Americans
to the **First Thanksgiving**, in 1621.

A Pilgrim asks a Native American king to Thanksgiving.

The Pilgrims give thanks for the new life in America.

Pilgrims and Native Americans at the First Thanksgiving

Word List

America (uh MER ih kuh)—The land that is now the United States

corn (KORN)—A tall plant and its kernels, which can be eaten

dirt (DIRT)—soil

First Thanksgiving (FURST thangks GIV ing)—The first feast of the Pilgrims and Native Americans

Mayflower (May flou er)—The ship on which the Pilgrims sailed in 1620

Native Americans (NAY tiv uh MER ih kunz)—Members of the peoples native to North America; American Indians

Pilgrims (PIL grimz)—People who settled in Plymouth, Massachusetts, in 1620

Books to Read

Bruchac, Joseph. *Squanto's Journey.* Silver Whistle, 2000.

Erickson, Paul. *Daily Life in the Pilgrim Colony, 1636.* Clarion Books, 2001.

Grace, Catherine O'Neill, Margaret Bruchac. *1621: A New Look at Thanksgiving.* National Geographic Society, 2001.

Waters, Kate. *Giving Thanks: The 1621 Harvest Feast.* Scholastic, 2001.

Websites to Visit

www.plimoth.org/Museum/museum.htm

www.tolatsga.org/wampa.html

http://teacher.scholastic.com/thanksgiving/interest.htm

http://members.aol.com/calebj/mayflower.html

http://pilgrims.net/plymouth/thanksgiving.htm

Index